This is the
Heart Work
of

_____

Copyright © 2018
Gail Carlock
Performance Publishing Group
McKinney, TX
All Worldwide Rights Reserved.

Gratitude is Transformational!

Encountering everyday moments with a contagious enthusiasm for life, seeking kindness in others and appreciating all we have releases power!

Passionate, transformative power that changes how we show up in our lives and how we experience our days.

Gratitude is a discipline, a choice to recognize, to record and to remember our Life moments.

Taking the time to reflect on what we are thankful for shows us that Gratitude is not a feeling.

It is an act of choosing to give thanks in all circumstances.

May your HeartWork Journal inspire and empower you to be, do and have a more Grateful life!

> Gratitude Equips, Empowers, & Inspires others to live TRANSFORMED lives!
> —Gail Carlock

Start each day with a GRATEFUL HEART!

Wherever you go,
go with all your HEART.
—Confucius

Let your LIGHT SHINE!

> My MISSION in life is not merely to survive, but to THRIVE!
> —Maya Angelou

What were you MADE to DO?

> Write it on your HEART
> that every day is the
> best day in the year!
> —Ralph Waldo Emerson

You make my HEART Happy!

> Among the things you can GIVE and still keep are your WORD, a SMILE & a GRATEFUL HEART!
> —Zig Ziglar

Hustle & HEART will set you apart!

Success DEMANDS singleness of PURPOSE!
—Vince Lombardi

Keep it SIMPLE!

GRATITUDE can TRANSFORM ordinary common days into THANKSGIVINGS...
—William Arthur Ward

Mighty HEART, strong will, intense focus!

Be HAPPY for this moment.
This moment is YOUR LIFE!
—Omar Khayyam

What's your NEXT Chapter?

LISTEN to your LIFE...
All the MOMENTS
are key moments!
—Frederick Buechner

GRATITUDE... That thing that
HOPES when your HEART is Full!

Life is not measured by the number of breaths we take, but by the moments that take our breath away.
—Maya Angelou

Some days you have to create your own SUNSHINE!

> You don't have to be GREAT to START, but you have to START to be GREAT!
> —Zig Ziglar

Are you Ready to Start?

Turn your WOUNDS into WISDOM!
—Oprah Winfrey

Don't walk through your toughest day alone. We're in this TOGETHER!

> In KINDergarten, I learned how to be KIND ... maybe I just need to get back to the BASICS.
> —Lisa Wilt

Abundance comes from a Simpler Life!

> The PLACE you are in
> needs YOU today!
> —Katherine Logan

You meet people for a Reason.
They are either a BLESSIN' or a LESSON!

> Don't be afraid to BE AMAZING!
> —Andy Offutt Irwin

Do the ONE Thing You love
more than anything in Life!

> The fastest way to SUCCESS is to replace BAD HABITS with GOOD HABITS.
> —Tom Ziglar

Be Patient ...
Sometimes you have to learn
the same thing OVER & OVER AGAIN!

Miracles happen to those who BELIEVE in them.
—Bernard Berensen

Believe in YOURSELF!

> Make every day
> a Work of HEART!
> —Gail Carlock

Get quiet & Listen to what is most important to you & run towards it with an open HEART.

> The bad news is TIME flies.
> The Good news is
> YOU are the PILOT.
> —Michael Altshuler

I think I will just be Happy today!

> Sometimes YOUR JOY is the source of your SMILE, but sometimes your SMILE is the source of YOUR JOY!
> —Thich Nhat Hanh

Anything is POSSIBLE!

> The biggest adventure YOU can take is to LIVE the LIFE of your DREAMS.
> —Oprah Winfrey

No excuses... Start Living!

> The key to effective GIVING is to stay open to RECEIVING!
> —Bob Burg

Simply LIVE a Good Life!

Vocabulary is vastly UNDERRATED!
—Gray Fleming

Words can SPEAK life!

Isn't it funny how day by day nothing CHANGES, but when you look back everything is DIFFERENT...
—C.S. Lewis

CELEBRATE Today!

If life were a book and I were the author, how would I want this STORY to END?
—Amy Purdy

Begin with the END in Mind!

> Know the value of TIME; snatch, seize and ENJOY every moment of it.
> —Lord Chesterfield

You were created to
Make a DIFFERENCE!

> Life will bring you pain all by itself. Your responsibility is to CREATE JOY!
> —Milton Erickson

Love & Gratitude give you LIFE!

LIFE is a Marvelous, Transitory ADVENTURE!
—Nikki Giovanni

Be your own definition of AMAZING!

*If you can IMAGINE it,
you can ACHIEVE it.
If you can DREAM it,
you can BECOME it.*
—William Arthur Ward

DREAM the impossible!

> Dedicate your life to a CAUSE greater than yourself, & your LIFE will become a GLORIOUS adventure.
> —Mack Douglas

Maximize your IMPACT!

> People don't buy WHAT you do.
> They buy WHY you do it!
> —Simon Sinek

People do business with those they know, like, & TRUST!

> Feed HOPE & people will FOLLOW you anywhere!
> —Libby Gill

Those who have HEART have HOPE!

> Positive ENERGY and positive PEOPLE create positive RESULTS.
> —Jon Gordon

Another Day, Another Chance to SPARKLE!

> The RIGHT Attitude very rarely LEADS to the Wrong ACTION!
> —Tom Ziglar

Are you READY to take ACTION?

HeartWork is CONTAGIOUS!
It Inspires Action &
Ignites GRATITUDE!
—Gail Carlock

What Ignites your GRATITUDE?

> SUCCESS is built sequentially.
> It's ONE THING at a time.
> —Gary Keller

Today sounds BETTER than someday!

> People don't decide their futures. They decide their HABITS, & their HABITS decide their FUTURES.
> —F.M. Alexander

How we spend our DAYS
is how we spend our LIVES!

> Your income is determined by how many people you SERVE and how well you SERVE them.
> —Bob Burg

Be the CHANGE!

...A Light HEART lives long.
—William Shakespeare

Love every MOMENT!

Your ATTITUDE,
not your APTITUDE,
will determine your ALTITUDE!
—Zig Ziglar

Enjoy the RIDE!

> The things you are PASSIONATE about are not random. They are your CALLING!
> —Fabienne Fredricksen

Fly to your DREAMS!

Love the life you have,
while you CREATE
the life of your DREAMS.
—Hal Elrod

This is your moment for a MIRACLE!

> We can dream, fail, and still SURVIVE!
> —Maya Angelou

If you want RAINBOWS,
you have to have RAIN!

There is a difference between giving DIRECTIONS & giving DIRECTION!
—Simon Sinek

Every experience is WORTH having!

And in the END, it's not the years in your life that COUNT; It's the LIFE in your years!
—Abraham Lincoln

Make the REST of your life,
the BEST of your life!

Love the LIFE you live.
LIVE the LIFE you love.
—Bob Marley

Think Happy. BE Happy!

> When you combine Love, Integrity, and Skill you Create LEGACY!
> —Tom Ziglar

Be a LEGACY Builder!

We RISE by lifting others!
—Rumi

You are BLESSED & LOVED!

Whether you think you can or think you can't, you're right.
—Henry Ford

Your thoughts MAKE your life!

Can you remember who you WERE before the World told you who you SHOULD BE?
—Danielle LaPorte

There is STILL time!

Be THANKFUL for what you have; you'll end up having more. If you concentrate on what you don't have, you will never, ever have enough.
—Oprah Winfrey

Gratitude unlocks the FULLNESS of life!

> Opportunity demands ownership. Sometimes you have to write CHECKS you are not sure you can CASH.
> —Gray Fleming

Stay HUMBLE. Work HARD. Be KIND!

Act as if what YOU DO makes a Difference.
It DOES!
—William James

What sets your HEART on Fire?

> Success is not a DESTINATION.
> It is a JOURNEY!
> —Zig Ziglar

Enjoy the JOURNEY!

> Where your treasure is, there is your HEART. Where your heart is, there is your HAPPINESS!
> —St. Augustine

Live from a GRATEFUL heart!

Only he who
can see the INVISIBLE
can do the IMPOSSIBLE!

—Frank L. Gaines

Keep the FAITH!

"People will forget what you SAID, people will forget what you DID, but people will NEVER forget how you made them FEEL."
—Maya Angelou

Vision is FAITH on FIRE!

> You are the AVERAGE of the FIVE people you SPEND the most TIME with.
> —Jim Rohn

Who are your Five Influencers?

You can't GIVE away what you don't POSSESS yourself.
—Rod Olson

In whom are you INVESTING?

> If your people are important, helping them UNDERSTAND why they specifically are critical to the overall mission is important, too.
> —Libby Gill

Are you a HOPE DRIVEN leader?

> Life is a DARING adventure, or it's NOTHING at ALL.
> —Helen Keller

What EXCITES your SOUL?

> The meaning of life is to FIND your GIFT. The purpose of life is to GIVE it away.
> —Author Unknown

Your STORY Matters!

Wear GRATITUDE like a cloak, & it will feed every corner of your LIFE!
—Rumi

Don't Let Anyone Steal your SPARKLE!

> I have failed Over & Over again in my LIFE. And that is WHY I SUCCEED!
> —Michael Jordan

Embrace Vulnerability!

> If you design your life GOALS first & BUILD your business around that VISION, you will avoid being a slave to your business!
> —Howard Partridge

Have you DESIGNED your life Goals?

> You make a LIVING by what you earn. You make a LIFE by what you GIVE.
> —Winston Churchill

Are YOU busy making a LIVING?

> I work very hard & I play very hard. I'm GRATEFUL for LIFE! And I live it. I BELIEVE life loves the LIVER of it! I LIVE it!
> —Maya Angelou

Experience LIFE ... Live it!

> To Handle yourself, use your head;
> to Handle others, use your HEART!
> —Eleanor Roosevelt

HeartWork Inspires!

Instead of GIVING something up,
TAKE something on!
—Rev. Patrick J. Miller

How do you define YOU?

> We CAN achieve what we can conceive & BELIEVE!
> —Mark Twain

A GOAL without a PLAN is just a wish!
—Antoine de Saint-Exupery

Life isn't about waiting for the STORM to pass. It's about learning how to DANCE in the rain!
—Vivian Greene

Today is a GIFT ... Make it COUNT!

Two roads diverged in a wood, and I took the one less traveled by, and that has made all the DIFFERENCE.
—Robert Frost

Every JOURNEY begins
with a Single step!

You MISS 100% of the SHOTS you don't Take!
—Wayne Gretzky

Life doesn't need to be PERFECT to be WONDERFUL!

> Our lives SUCCEED or FAIL gradually, then Suddenly, one CONVERSATION at a time!
> —Susan Scott

The Conversation is the RELATIONSHIP!

> Life is too short to live an ORDINARY life. Start living an EXTRAORDINARY life!
> —Michelle Prince

Do YOU want more for your LIFE?

> Life is 10% of what HAPPENS to me and 90% of how I REACT to it!
> —Charles Swindoll

Create your own SUNSHINE!

What would you ATTEMPT to do if you knew YOU could not Fail?

—Anonymous

Be Adventurous, Life is Short!

The DIFFICULTY in Life is in the CHOICE!
—George Moore

What does your BEHAVIOR SAY about YOU?

> Set yourself earnestly to DISCOVER what you are made to do, and then GIVE yourself PASSIONATELY to the doing of it.
> —Martin Luther King, Jr.

Are you a GOOD FINDER?

Follow your WISHING HEART!
—Lisa Loeb

Let your HEART SOAR!

You CAN have everything in life you WANT, if you will just HELP other people get what they want.
—Zig Ziglar

Relationships MATTER!

Transform Your Thoughts.
Transform Your Life.

Gail Carlock, Owner and CEO of HEARTWORK Inspires, with her 28 years of Medical Device Leadership and Sales Experience, lives her Passion and Purpose. Gail is a Ziglar Certified Trainer, who has worked with companies like Dupont, Guidant, Medtronic, St. Jude and Abbott helping their teams have transparent conversations that drive results and impact lives.

Gail is a future focused, hope based, energy engager, who speaks greatness to others. HeartWork Inspires focuses on capturing the Hearts of individuals and teams, while holding them Able!

Maximize Your Impact!

www.ingramcontent.com/pod-product-compliance
Lightning Source LLC
Chambersburg PA
CBHW022108090426
42743CB00008B/770